Drawing on his broad expertise as a biblical scholar, and in his trademark, accessible style, Ben Witherington nimbly takes us to core features of the biblical portrayal of God via the nouns that express God's character. There is much here to inform, correct, and inspire the Christian mind, and this rich homily is spiced with sufficient theological controversy to keep the reader wide awake!

JOHN BARCLAY
The University of Durham, England

Here is a thoughtful collection of meditations on God's character—with clearly-drawn implications for the character of those who claim to belong to such a God—by a scholar-pastor whose love for God, Scripture, and church shines through every chapter. Along the way, he healthfully challenges all of his readers, sometimes quite directly, to examine even firmly held theological convictions afresh in light of the scriptural testimony to God's character. While rightly admitting that knowing God fully lies beyond our capacity on this side of eternity, Witherington has not relaxed his own efforts, and would not have us slacken in our own, to think right thoughts of God and thus love, serve, and reflect God ever more fully.

DAVID A. DESILVA
Ashland Theological Seminary

Ben Witherington is justly famous as a superb Biblical scholar. In *Who God Is*, he summarizes that extensive learning and reflection in a form that is simple, approachable, and understandable, aimed as much at lay people as at clergy and academics. Anyone interested in Christianity will profit from this rich, concise, book.

PHILIP JENKINS
Baylor University

Saints, seekers, and skeptics alike have posed and pondered the question, "Who is God?" Ben Witherington III offers a thoughtful, accessible, and successful introduction to *Who God Is*. Witherington's meditations on God's multi-faceted, many-splendored character allow readers to see anew that the God of Abraham, Isaac, Jacob and the God and Father of our Lord Jesus Christ is a God of love, light, life, spirit; is One with the Son and the Holy Spirit; and is great and greatly to be praised. I especially commend Ben's book to those who have taken God for granted or have taken for granted that there is no God.

TODD D. STILL
Baylor University

Excellent works about the character of God are rare these days, especially those that lead us into careful biblical reflection about Him. *Who God Is* takes you there. In this focused look at some core attributes of God, you will be reminded of just how glorious our holy God of grace and compassion is.

DARRELL BOCK
Dallas Theological Seminary

Ben Witherington seeks to address an imbalance in Christian thinking about God, in which adjectives like holy and righteous are often discussed but nouns like love, light, and life are not. Intended for general readers, *Who is God* succeeds in clarifying God's moral character, which ultimately undergirds theology and worship. Witherington rightly emphasizes that it is especially in the incarnation that God's love, light, Spirit, and life are so clearly revealed.

CRAIG A. EVANS
Houston Baptist University

Ben Witherington discusses Scripture with the sort of eagerness that makes you want to do likewise. I'll not think of the themes of God as love, light, light and one without also thinking of this little book that unpacks those biblical themes so thoroughly.

JASON BYASSEE
Vancouver School of Theology, British Columbia

This study by Ben Witherington III shows how we as follow-ers of Jesus can sometimes focus too much on the things that describe God instead of putting our focus on who God *is*. God *is* love. God *is* light. God *is* life. These, and many others, are all things God *is*, not just words that describe His character. Ben's decision to shift our perspective away from descriptive adjectives to nouns (grammar nerds everywhere, rejoice!), is an important one. This study will stretch how you think about who God is, allowing us to take another look at who we believe God really is in our own lives. Whether you've been following Jesus for years or you've just decided to give this Christian thing a try, I would encourage you to go through Ben's study. I prom-ise his words will not only change the way you think about God, but also shape your relationship with Him for years to come.

ADAM WEBER
Embrace Church

This book reminded me of who God really is. In it, I learned that the world's desperate need today is really to really know God. God is love. God is light. God is life. Instead of trying to get more love, light, and life into the world, I am going to focus on getting more God into the world! As a pastor and church leader, this was the most important book I have read this year. It will be for you too.

JACOB ARMSTRONG
Providence Church, Mt. Juliet, TN

When many folks say "God," they don't know what they are talking about, or at least they are not talking about the God who meets us in Scripture as Jesus Christ. For decades, Ben Witherington has been helping the rest of us love Scripture. In this lively, instructive book, Ben helps us to marvel at the various names of God in Scripture. You'll pray, worship, and maybe—by the grace of God, after Ben has helped you—call upon the God who has called to us in Christ.

WILL WILLIMON
Duke Divinity School

To those who have followed Ben's work for a while, we already know him as one gifted in helping the deep truths of Scripture find a clearer understanding in our minds and a more welcome home in our hearts. And *Who God Is* is no exception to what we've come to expect. Open the cover for yourself, discover all the promise and power contained within the names of God, and be reminded again why so many of us look forward to practicing what Ben preaches!

E. DALE LOCKE
Community of Hope Church, Southeast Florida

WHO
GOD IS

WHO
GOD IS

Meditations *on the*
Character *of* Our God

BEN WITHERINGTON III

LEXHAM PRESS

Who God Is: Meditations on the Character of Our God

Copyright 2020 Ben Witherington III

Lexham Press, 1313 Commercial St., Bellingham, WA 98225
LexhamPress.com

Unless otherwise noted, Scripture quotations are the author's translation or are from the Holy Bible, New International Version®, NIV®. Copyright ©1973, 1978, 1984, 2011 by Biblica, Inc.™ Used by permission of Zondervan.

Print ISBN 9781683593645
Digital ISBN 9781683593652
Library of Congress Control Number 2019956735

Lexham Editorial: Abigail Stocker, Allisyn Ma, Sarah Awa
Cover Design: Christine Christophersen
Typesetting: Sarah Vaughan

CONTENTS

ACKNOWLEDGMENTS

This book is dedicated in memoriam to the two men who most influenced my early thinking about God— C. S. Lewis and Dr. Bernard Boyd, my Bible professor at UNC-Chapel Hill. I was not yet a teenager in 1963 when Lewis died on the same day as John F. Kennedy, but his *Mere Christianity* and *The Screwtape Letters* made an early impact on me. Dr. Boyd also left us too soon (in 1975) after twenty-five years of being the James A. Gray Professor of Biblical Studies and guiding thousands of us toward a love for the Bible and also a ministry or career of teaching it. I was fortunate to have graduated in 1974 and to have taken all his classes. I would not be who I am today nor would I have chosen the career I've had were it not for these two wonderful Christian men.

Apologies to Dr. Boyd: I know you wanted me to go to Princeton, and I did do summer study there with your classmate Bruce Metzger, but I felt strongly called to go to Gordon-Conwell, and their New Testament faculty (Scholer, Michaels, Lincoln, and Fee) was second to none at the time for an evangelical like me.

A special thanks to my former TA and doctoral student, Joy Vaughan, who contributed the reflection and study questions after each chapter.

CHRISTMAS 2019

"The great thing to remember is that, though our feelings come and go, His love for us does not."

—C. S. Lewis,
Mere Christianity

PROLOGUE
THE STARTING POINT

Something has bothered me for a long time. I'm referring to the fact that even devout Christians seem to place far more emphasis on the adjectives applied to God in the Bible than on the nouns. This is not to say that the adjectives are not vitally important—God is almighty; God is righteous; God is holy; God is merciful; God is compassionate, and so on. But frankly, nouns are more important than adjectives when it comes to the character of any sentient being—whether we are talking about God or angels or human beings.

That God is *love* tells us something very different than saying we have a *loving* God. That God is life is different than saying God is living or lively. That God is light is different than saying God is enlightening. You see my point. Too often we emphasize the adjectives without fully taking in the implications of the nouns. In this particular book, I intend to rectify this problem as best I can.[1]

Consider the matter from another angle. As I stressed in my earlier study *The Indelible Image*,[2] the connecting point between our theology and our ethics as Christians comes from the fact that we are created in God's image, which is to say that our character and behavior should mirror God's character and behavior, though on a lesser scale. "Be ye holy; for I am holy," says the Bible (1 Pet 1:16 KJV; see also Lev 11:44). Working backward, we may ask, "Why is the Great Commandment to love God with all your being and your neighbor as yourself? Why does Paul say that love is even greater than faith or hope in 1 Corinthians 13? Why is "love" the first of the fruits

---

1. Here a clarification of things is in order. I am not talking about God's divine essence or whether Jesus is divine, nor am I talking about God's divine attributes of being omni-everything as only God can be. I am rather talking about God's moral character—a character he wants replicated in us by means of redemption. I am asking and answering: What kind of persons are Father, Son, and Spirit?

2. This two-volume work was published by InterVarsity Press in 2009–2010. See also my *Biblical Theology: The Convergence of the Canon* (Cambridge University Press, 2019).

of the Spirit in Galatians 5?" (I could go on.) My conclusion is that what God most requires of us and most
wants us to manifest in all our relationships (including
with our enemies) is that which most characterizes the
very nature of God—love.

Most of us are familiar with 1 John 4:8 and 16, which
states unequivocally, "Whoever does not love does not
know God, because God is love. ... Whoever lives in love
lives in God, and God in them." That seems to be clear
enough, but what happens when we make "God is love"
into our starting point for reflecting on the character of
God? Since we must take into account all that the Bible
says, I will hasten to add that God's love is a holy love,
which is markedly distinct from human love as we often
use the term. God's holiness is not without love, and
he's not love without holiness; indeed, the very essence
of holiness is love—a love that transforms sinners into
"holy ones" or saints. We will explore "God is love" in
our first chapter in this study, followed by chapters on
the other major nouns used of God.[3] Let's get started!

---

3. These are basically the only significant nouns applied to God in the Bible,
hence the focus on them.

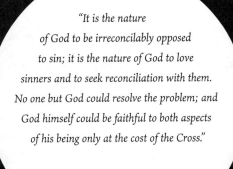

"It is the nature
of God to be irreconcilably opposed
to sin; it is the nature of God to love
sinners and to seek reconciliation with them.
No one but God could resolve the problem; and
God himself could be faithful to both aspects
of his being only at the cost of the Cross."

—C. K. BARRETT, *THE EPISTLE
TO THE ROMANS*

CHAPTER 1
GOD IS LOVE

M y college Bible professor at UNC-Chapel Hill, Dr. Bernard Boyd, was a medic and chaplain in World War II in the Pacific theater. He once told a riveting story of rushing to the aid of a fallen young soldier who was badly wounded and about to pass into eternity. Dr. Boyd administered morphine to ease the pain, and the young man looked up into Dr. Boyd's eyes and said, "You are our chaplain. Surely you must know. What is God like?" Dr. Boyd quickly assured the young man that God was like Christ and was a loving and forgiving Father. The young man passed away with that assurance in his heart.

I take it as axiomatic that the clearest revelation of God's character comes to us in Christ and as a result of the Christ event. In doing Christian theology, it is always wise to work from the clearest revelation to the more obscure. I also take it as axiomatic that there are paradoxes about God's character that we shall never resolve because "we know in part" (1 Cor 13:9). Doing theology should always be an exercise in recognizing that we understand God and we know God *only partially*. Unlike God, we are not omniscient, and what we do know stretches our capacities to the breaking point. In other words, before doing theology, one should get up each morning and take a humility pill and perhaps recite the Pauline doxology:

> Oh, the depth of the riches of the wisdom and
> knowledge of God!
>> How unsearchable his judgments,
>> and his paths beyond tracing out!
> "Who has known the mind of the Lord?
>> Or who has been his counselor?"
> "Who has ever given to God,
>> that God should repay him?"
> For from him and through him and for him are
> all things.
>> To him be the glory forever! Amen.
> (Rom 11:33–38)

LEAD WITH LOVE

Let me start by saying that to assert "God is love" is by no means the same as saying "love is my god." In the first place, the word "love" in our affective culture unfortunately primarily refers to a feeling, a desire, or an activity, such as lovemaking. The sentence "God is love" in Scripture refers instead to the very character of God, which is not to deny that our God is often passionate about things. As A. J. Heschel used to say, the biblical God is a God of pathos; he is not the "unmoved mover" of all things.[1]

In its core character as an action, love must be freely given and freely received. It cannot be coerced, and it cannot be predetermined or else it is not love. Inherent in love is a measure of *freedom*. One can be wooed, one can be persuaded, one can be led to love, but one cannot be forced to love.

What that means in a sentence like "God is love" is that God is a free agent. He is not compelled or even bound by his own nature to love. No, God chooses to love because it is consistent with and a natural expression of

---

1. See A. J. Heschel's classic study, *The Prophets* (New York: Harper, 2001).

his very character. Especially when it comes to sinners, even notorious sinners, God has no obligation either by nature or by contract to love such people, but he chooses to do so because that is a true expression of who God is, and that is why we talk about God's love as "pure grace," as unmerited favor or blessing. Let's turn now to 1 John 4:7–21.[2] Here is the full text:

> Dear friends, let us love one another, for love comes from God. Everyone who loves has been born of God and knows God. Whoever does not love does not know God, because God is love. This is how God showed his love among us: He sent his one and only Son into the world that we might live through him. This is love: not that we loved God, but that he loved us and sent his Son as an atoning sacrifice for our sins. Dear friends, since God so loved us, we also ought to love one another. No one has ever seen God; but if we love

---

2. For a much more detailed and exegetical study of this material, see Witherington, *Letters and Homilies for Hellenized Christians*, Vol. 1 (Downers Grove: InterVarsity Press, 2006), 517–34.

one another, God lives in us and his love is made complete in us.

This is how we know that we live in him and he in us: He has given us of his Spirit. And we have seen and testify that the Father has sent his Son to be the Savior of the world. If anyone acknowledges that Jesus is the Son of God, God lives in them and they in God. And so we know and rely on the love God has for us.

God is love. Whoever lives in love lives in God, and God in them. This is how love is made complete among us so that we will have confidence on the day of judgment: In this world we are like Jesus. There is no fear in love. But perfect love drives out fear, because fear has to do with punishment. The one who fears is not made perfect in love.

We love because he first loved us. Whoever claims to love God yet hates a brother or sister is a liar. For whoever does not love their brother and sister, whom they have seen, cannot love God, whom they have not seen. And he has given us this

command: Anyone who loves God must also love
their brother and sister.

First John 4:7–21 can be called a rhetorical unit, and it
begins with perhaps the most love-filled verse in the
whole of the Scriptures. The audience is called "beloved"
(*agapetoi*), and we have the verb *agapomen* as well as the
noun *agape*, even the participle *ho agapon*. The Beloved
Disciple is telling us that love describes the very character
of God, and it is supposed to describe the very character
of Christians and the very nature of Christian community.

Doubtless, the Beloved Disciple is emphasizing this
because of the recent splits and rancor in the community
to which he is writing. That sort of behavior is antithetical to modeling the character of God. Notice as well that
while there are a variety of Greek words for "love," we
do not find *eros* used here or even the terms usually used
to describe brotherly or sisterly or even familial love. No,
here the author is stressing that the Christian community
should be manifesting and modeling the very character,
the very love ascribed to God himself.

Needless to say, where one starts in describing the character of God, what one thinks is *most* fundamental about our God, will affect how we view God's attributes—such as God's sovereignty and his righteousness. Is there something more fundamental we could say about God's character (not merely his omni-everything nature or attributes as the only living God) than that God is love? I don't think so, and neither did the one who was called Jesus' Beloved Disciple.

The next thing to notice is that we are told when *agape* love is manifested among and between human beings that this has come from God himself. The Beloved Disciple essentially says love like that is of God. It doesn't occur of its own accord among fallen human beings. Stephen Smalley stresses that a transformation of a fallen human being is required for *agape* to be manifested by us: "Anyone who enters into a real relationship with a loving God can be transformed into a loving person."[3] But there is even more. Our author is claiming that by receiving and being transformed by the love of God, we come to know God as he actually is.

---

3. S. S. Smalley, *1, 2, and 3 John*, Vol. 51 (Word, 1984), 238.

The author is willing to say the opposite as well: that those who do not manifest *agape* love do not know God. Again, this begins to make sense of why loving God with all our being is part of the Great Commandment, why Paul says love is even greater than faith or hope, and why love is mentioned first as a fruit of the Spirit. God is a lover. God wants to transform us into loving people (again, in the *agape* sense of the word), and above all, he wants us to manifest this aspect of the divine character in our lives not only in response to God, but in the way we relate to our fellow human beings. This becomes all too obvious later, in 1 John 4, when the Beloved Disciple stresses that if you hate your fellow Christians, then you don't truly love God. While this discourse is all about relationships within the Christian community (and we need to bear in mind that our author is using powerful rhetoric to make his points), he is not exaggerating here. Elsewhere Jesus will redefine what it means to be a neighbor to those who are not followers of Christ and will even call for us to love and forgive our enemies. That, however, is not the focus in 1 John 4.

AVOIDING SLOPPY *AGAPE*

It becomes evident that our author is referring to a special sort of godly Christian love here if we do a detailed study of the use of the term *agape* both in the New Testament and elsewhere in Greek literature.[4] C. H. Dodd helps clarify this when he says:

> The noun is scarcely found in non-Biblical Greek. The verb [*agapeo*] generally has such meanings as "to be content with," "to like," "to esteem," "to prefer." It is a comparatively cool and colorless word. It is this word, with its noun, that the translators of the Old Testament [into Greek, i.e., the LXX] used by preference for the love of God to man and man's response, and by doing so they began to fill it with the distinctive content for which paganism, even in its highest forms, had no proper expression. In the New Testament this fresh content is enlarged

---

4. The definitive study was done long ago by Ceslas Spicq, *Agape in the New Testament*, 3 vols. (Herder: 1963). Also helpful is C. S. Lewis's *The Four Loves*, (Nelson, 2005).

and intensified through the meditation upon the meaning of the death of Christ."[5]

When the pagans do clear their throats and talk about God's love, which is a rarity, they choose to use a very different word (*eros*), which normally refers to sexual desire and sexual love. This is in part because many of the ancients conceived of the gods as very much like human beings, only with a good deal more power. The thought process in 1 John flows in the opposite direction—not "the gods are rather like us" but "we must become like the one and only living God, who is *agape*." The God of the Bible is wholly other, a creator and redeemer God who does not take his cues from human beings or their behavior but rather creates them and redeems them into his very image, manifesting his character. In short, we do not define God; God defines us. God is the very definition of what love means.

The Beloved Disciple is not trying here to define God by means of an abstraction like "love," a word which can have many meanings and implications in English. Dodd

---

5. C. H. Dodd, *The Johannine Epistles* (London: Hodder, 1946), 111–12.

puts it this way: "If the characteristic divine activity is that of loving, then God must be personal, for we cannot be loved by an abstraction, or by anything less than a person. … [But to say] 'God is love' implies that all his activity is loving activity. If he creates, he creates in love; if he rules, he rules in love; if he judges, he judges in love. All that he does is the expression of his nature which is—to love."[6]

THE PARADOX

Then what will seem to us a total paradox, or even an oxymoron, comes into view; exhibit A of the loving character of God toward human beings: God sends his only and unique Son to die for an ungrateful and sinful world. God's love and loving is proactive, not merely reactive. It is fully expressed in his salvation plan and the execution of that plan in Christ. But the death of Christ reveals not only the profound love of God for humankind but also one of God's fundamental traits. He is holy; he is righteous; and he cannot pass over sins forever, as Paul reminds us (see Rom 3). God is not a being that exercises one aspect of his character at the expense of the others—not even

---

6. Dodd, *Johannine Epistles*, 109–10.

in the case of love. God's love is always a holy love. Not love without holiness and not holiness and righteousness without love—thank goodness, or none of us could stand or have a positive relationship with God.

Notice that in 1 John 4:9–10 God sent his Son so that we might have everlasting life through him, but he also sent him as an atoning sacrifice for sin. If God is love, then no wonder a holy God is also righteously angry about our sin and must do something about it if we are to be reconciled to him. After all, it is sin that has destroyed our relationship with our loving God, just as sin destroys our relationships with other human beings. Love and life are the antitheses of hate and death, and yet the substitutionary sacrifice, the atoning death of Christ, is the prime example of God's love for us.

While various scholars, including notably C. H. Dodd, have tried hard to read the terms *hilasmos/hilasterion* as referring only to expiation rather than also to propitiation, this is a costly mistake because it misconstrues the very character of God. Yes, God wants us to be "expiated," cleansed of our sin and the guilt that accrues with it, but there can be no expiation unless God's demand for "propitiation" (for righteousness and justice) is also satisfied. One characteristic of God cannot be raised above another. God's *full* character was expressed on the cross.

Put another way, unless Christ's death on the cross was absolutely necessary for the righteous demands of a righteous God to be fulfilled and yet salvation to be offered, God is in no sense a loving God. What sort of Father would demand his only and beloved Son submit to crucifixion unless it was the one essential and sufficient means to save the world? But then, if it was both essential and sufficient for salvation to be offered to all, paradoxically the cross becomes the epitome of God's love for us all. As I once put it in a Lenten poem entitled "RSVP," "God's ways are not our ways / our eyes cannot see / the logic of love / nailed to a tree." Long ago, James Denny put it far more eloquently than I could:

> So far from finding any kind of contrast between love and propitiation, the apostle can convey no idea of love to any one except by pointing to the propitiation—love is what is manifested there. ... For him, to say "God is love" is exactly the same

as to say "God has in His Son made atonement for the sin of the world." If the propitiatory death of Jesus is eliminated from the love of God, it might be unfair to say the love of God is robbed of all meaning, but it is certainly robbed of its apostolic meaning. It no longer has that meaning which goes deeper than sin, sorrow, and death, and which recreates life in the adoring joy, wonder, and purity of the first Epistle of St. John.[7]

Longtime New Testament professor Gerald Hawthorne named Philippians 2:5–11 as his favorite New Testament text. He translated two of the key lines of that text as follows: "Precisely because he was in very nature God, he did not choose to exploit his equality with God [the Father], but rather emptied himself." In other words, God by nature—by his very character—is self-sacrificial, not self-centered or self-indulgent. This totally accords with what the Beloved Disciple has in mind when he says God

---

7. J. Denny, *The Death of Christ* (Tyndale, 1951), 152.

is love. God's love is self-sacrificial. It's not about protecting his rights or honor.[8]

It is interesting and important that this little rhetorical unit in 1 John 4 works to the conclusion: since God loves us to this extent and in this way, we should love other believers in this way. We might have expected him to say, "Since God does this, we should reciprocate and love God in the same way." This, however, is to forget how integrally theology and ethics are connected in the canon. The Great Commandment does command us to love God with our whole being, but in the same breath, it says we must love our neighbor as ourselves.

God's love is the instigator, the enabler, of genuine human love. God as a lover enables human beings to truly love—to love self-sacrificially, to love virtuously, to love supernaturally rather than merely naturally. John Painter helps us understand that God does not merely model love; he pours his love into us so that we might properly love: "God's love is definitive, primary, and the source of all

---

8. Gregg Okesson, my colleague at Asbury who was one of Gerald's students at Wheaton, says Gerry emphasized this point and this passage over and over again.

[real] love. In arguing this way the author implies ... that human love is seen to be derivative and responsive. This implies that human love continually needs to be redefined and corrected by divine love because human love in the world has the potential to be corrupted."[9]

LOVE CASTS OUT FEAR

When believers love one another, the love God has poured into them comes to completion or is brought to its most perfect expression and has its full intended effect (cf. 1 John 2:5; 3:17). God is not interested in merely loving isolated individuals; he is interested in creating community, the family of faith, through his love. God's perfect love in us comes to fruition when we love one another as we are loved. And notice that this love has a purging effect: It casts out fear—fear of the wrath of a righteous God; fear of our fellow humans, which leads us to isolate and protect ourselves from them; fear of circumstances beyond our control.

---

9. J. Painter, *1, 2, and 3 John* (Collegeville: Liturgical Press, 2002), 267.

If the God who is love is also the almighty God, then fear, while a "normal" human emotion and reaction to life in a world full of harm and evil and suffering, becomes the opposite of faith in that loving God. There are few things sadder than to see Christians live their lives on the basis of fear-based rather than faith- and love-based thinking. This is not due to a lack of fearsome things in the world. It is because the loving God has overcome the world, overcome sin and death through the sacrifice of his Son, Jesus Christ. As so often is the case, while we may *affirm* the truths of Scripture, we do not always understand or live out the implications of that truth in the ways we relate (or fail to relate) to one another. The Beloved Disciple writes this discourse to correct not only our understanding of God as love but also the ethical and behavioral implications of that truth.

WERE WE PREDESTINED TO LOVE?

One of the major implications of what I have said in this chapter about God's love is that it means that certain readings of the language about predestination, election, and salvation are likely to be wrong. Let's consider for a moment one of the major bones of contention, Romans 8:28–30.[10]

> And we know that in all things God works for the good of those who love him, who have been called according to his purpose [choice]. For those God foreknew he also predestined to be conformed to the image of his Son, that he might be the first-born among many brothers and sisters. And those he predestined, he also called; those he called, he also justified; those he justified, he also glorified.

The first thing to note about this text is that it includes a rarity; it talks about those who love God. Normally, Paul talks about God's love for human beings, not the reverse, which is what we find here. The second thing to notice, which was noticed long ago by John Chrysostom, is that the word "his" does not figure into the Greek text of these verses. Paul simply says "according to choice" or less possibly, "according to purpose." The question that should be

---

10. On all of what follows and much more, one should consult Witherington and D. Hyatt, *Paul's Letter to the Romans* (Grand Rapids: Eerdmans, 2004).

asked is: Whose choice or purpose? Granted, the calling is done by God in this statement, but it is not as clear who is doing the choosing. Remember, the subject is not simply God, but rather God and those who love God, and Paul does not say here *how* those persons came to love God. Doubtless, God called them to do so, but calling is not choosing, much less predestining. Elsewhere—for instance, two chapters later, in Romans 10—Paul states clearly that people come to faith in the biblical God and his Christ through hearing the preaching of the good news and responding in faith.

This leads to the question of whether one has noticed that the Greek word *ous* at the beginning of verse 29 refers back to "those who love God and are called." In other words, verse 29 is not telling us how non-Christians become Christians; it is speaking to us about how those who love God have a wonderful destiny: to be conformed to the image of Christ. This was God's plan all along for those who love him, so much so that those whom he knew in advance would love him, he destined to be conformed to the image of his Son.[11]

---

11. For a helpful study of love as a major theme in the Bible, see Patrick

Nothing here suggests an arbitrary choosing of some individuals from a mass of unredeemed humanity to be saved. No, God's calling was responded to in love, and even before they did respond in love, God had in mind destining them to be conformed to the image of Christ through, first of all, being in right relationship with God or "righteoused," sanctified, and finally glorified when full conformity to the image of Christ by means of resurrection transpires. The plan, the calling, the initiative is entirely with God, and this passage is written the way it is to reassure those who love God that God will indeed work all things together for good for them. He has a wonderful plan and future in mind for them.

Paul does not say everything he thinks is true about this matter here; rather, he makes clear that God is involved in the whole process from before the start of someone loving God to the glorification of that person. He reassures them as well that neither third parties nor circumstances can rip them out of the firm grasp that God has on their lives. This does not mean that apostasy is impossible for the

Mitchel's *The Message of Love: The Only Thing that Counts* (Downers Grove: InterVarsity Press, 2019).

Christian—something he rightly warns about elsewhere (see Gal 5:16–21)—but that is not the intention of this passage.

ELECTION IS NOT SALVATION

It is equally clear if you read Romans 8 in tandem with Romans 9–11 that the following is true about Paul's view on this subject: His concept of election is corporate. Think of Israel in the Old Testament and Christ in the New Testament (Christ is the quintessential chosen one or elect one of God); election has to do with the historical purposes of God, rather than with the notion of personal salvation. This ought to be evident when one considers that: (1) many chosen or elect Israelites committed apostasy and did not end up either saved or entering the promised land, and (2) Christ, the truly elect or chosen one of God, never needed to be saved, and (3) the person called "my anointed one" in Isaiah turns out to be an unsaved, non-monotheistic person named Cyrus the Persian (Isa 45:1). In short, election for a historical purpose is one thing; individual salvation is another.

A further thing that comes to light from what follows in Romans 9–11 is that God foreknows both things he wants to happen and things he doesn't. God knows all possibilities as well as all actualities, and in many cases, he is the actor who turns the possible into the actual, but this is not so in the case of his foreknowing sin or evil. Foreknowing is not the same thing as destining in advance. Still further, God wants the full number of gentiles to be saved and also "all Israel" to be saved (Rom 11:26). He's not talking about an elect *few* being saved. That was never God's desire or plan.

It is also true that this loving God knows not all will be saved. One has to ask why. The short answer Paul gives is that some have hardened or fit themselves for judgment, and others have been conformed to the image of Christ through the work of God in their lives by responding and continuing to respond to the call and work of God for and in them. For them, "all things will be worked together for good" (Rom 8:28).

This reading of Romans 8–11 makes sense when we realize once more that love involves freedom. Paul stresses this freedom when he speaks to Christians about avoiding sin: "You, my brothers and sisters, were called to be free. But do not use your freedom to indulge the flesh; rather, serve one another humbly in love" (Gal 5:13). Notice how Paul assumes that freedom is necessary to love and serve others, but it can also be used to sinful ends as well.

Yes, love is freely given and freely responded to by grace through faith. Not grace without faith, and none of the above without love given and love received and responded to freely. It is God's grace that enables the loving response, but still the response is voluntary, not predetermined. God's grace, like God's love, treats us as persons who, with the aid of grace, have the power of contrary choice. Our God is not the "godfather," making us an offer of salvation we can't refuse.

A PROPHETIC WORD ON
GOD'S CHARACTER

Consider for a moment the beautiful passage in Hosea 11, which begins:

> When Israel was a child, I loved him,[12]
>   and out of Egypt I called my son.

---

12. The word here for "love" is *ahav*, not *hesed*. This is of importance because Yahweh is not talking about a kind of "covenant love" he owes to his chosen ones, at least when they are faithful. He's talking about the very nature of God who loves in spite of the infidelities of Israel.

In this prophetic poem, Hosea tells us that God is like a loving parent who is distraught over the waywardness of his children. What shall he do about it? Shall he snap his fingers and destine them to return to him? No! He woos them back by explaining his nature; he is not quixotic or changeable. He loves even when love is not returned, even when the opposite of love characterizes his people. God, in his character, is emphatically not like changeable human beings, including his chosen people. "Love is not love / Which alters when it alteration finds. … / O no! it is an ever-fixed mark," as Shakespeare would say.[13]

The Hosea passage ends with Yahweh portrayed as a mighty lion roaring, calling to his cubs to return. Throughout the passage, God is depicted as loving, merciful, good—in short, as "light," in the full theological and ethical sense of that term.[14] (We will look at light more in the next chapter.)

---

13. William Shakespeare, "Sonnet 116."

14. Remembering the words of Lewis in *The Lion, the Witch and the Wardrobe* where the question is asked if Aslan, the great lion, is safe. "'Course he isn't safe," comes the reply. "But he is good!"

WHAT ABOUT GOD'S SOVEREIGNTY?

At this point, I normally hear the objection, "Don't you believe in God's sovereignty?" Actually, I strongly affirm that God is omnipotent, but the question is: How does God exercise his power and sovereignty?[15] In my view, God is the dominant actor in the universe, and in some things, he is the *only* actor. For example, the Hebrew word *bara* ("to create") is solely predicated of God in the Old Testament and for good reason. He created the universe and all that is in it *by himself.* Furthermore, as we have seen in Romans 8, God's hand is still on the whole historical process such that Paul can say God works everything together for good for those who love him (Rom 8:28). God is not the watchmaker God of the deists, who think that God set all of creation in motion and then sat back and left it to its own devices and natural processes. This is clearly not the view of the biblical writers. God

---

15. Here is where I would differ from a Reformed theologian like John Piper not on God's divine power or other attributes of his divinity, but on God's character. We do not agree on the nature of God's love, grace, nor on the scope of that redeeming love. John 3:16 was telling the truth when it said God loves the fallen world of humanity and sent his Son to redeem, not condemn, that world.

is involved everywhere and all the time, particularly on behalf of those who love him.

One final question is appropriate in this chapter: If God is truly good, truly omnipotent, and truly loving, why is there evil in the world?

God set up the universe with other sentient, intelligent beings—namely, angels and humans—who have a modicum of free choice. This is hardly surprising, since God is love and he desired his creatures to love him freely. Some respond positively, and some do not. But God is *not* the author of sin or evil. There are secondary causes in the world that produce sin and evil: human beings and angelic beings, according to the Bible. This is not God's will for their lives or anyone's lives. Sin and evil are violations of God's will. We live in a fallen world, which we human beings cause with the help of the powers of darkness.

Love requires some freedom of expression—real freedom, not merely feeling like one is free or not compelled.[16]

---

16. On which Jonathan Edwards, *The Works of Jonathan Edwards*, Vol. 1, *The Freedom of the Will*, (Yale University Press, 2009), has much to say. It turns out what Edwards means by freedom *isn't* the power of contrary choice; it's just that we don't *feel* compulsed, even though we could not have chosen otherwise. It is odd that on the one hand he wants to say God's grace is powerful, even "irresistible," and on the other hand, even though God's mercy is over all his works, his grace is not sufficient

If there is genuine freedom—the power of contrary choice to God's will for angels and humans—there will always be the possibility that wrong choices can be made. We and some of the angelic beings are responsible for the sin and evil in this world. Not God. Furthermore, God cannot be tempted, and he tempts no one. God is light, and in him is no darkness at all, which brings us to the topic of our next chapter.

REFLECTIONS

Imagine a world in which love is perfectly displayed, a humanity that is free to make the loving choice and always does. It is hard to imagine, isn't it? *God is love*, as a descriptor of God's character, offers an alternative track for building one's perception of God. In every work of God, he is love. Even in punishment for sin, he is love. His love is not altered when humanity, in its freedom, chooses to sin against him. Instead, he acts in love to correct and redeem.

When starting with love, one may quickly realize God's desire to be in community with his creation. But this is not the end-all, be-all goal. Rather, he intends Christians

to enable a person to freely respond to the gospel.

to reflect his loving character to one another. We must remember, though, that we are not in this alone. Romans 5 aptly fills in how we can love as "God's love has been poured out into our hearts through the Holy Spirit, who has been given to us." As a result, no self-help program will truly inspire us to love. It is God himself who is love and who pours love into us so that we may truly love one another.

STUDY QUESTIONS

- Why did we start with "God is love"?

- What role does "a measure of freedom" play in understanding God's character as love?

- What does 1 John 4 reveal about God's character?

- How does God's love impact our ability to love?

- How does understanding the definition of "God is love" change discussions of predestination, election, and salvation? Give specific examples.

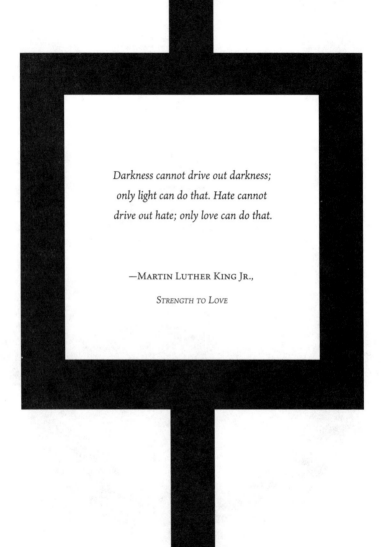

Darkness cannot drive out darkness;
only light can do that. Hate cannot
drive out hate; only love can do that.

—MARTIN LUTHER KING JR.,

STRENGTH TO LOVE

CHAPTER 2
GOD IS LIGHT

I t is an interesting fact that while God the Father is called "love" in the Johannine tradition and Jesus is not, both God and Jesus are called "light" in this same tradition (the Gospel of John and 1 John). Throughout the Fourth Gospel, it is Jesus who is mainly called the "light" (3:19–21; 8:12; 9:3–5; 11:9–10; 12:35–36; 12:46). We do find the idea that Jesus was considered to be a light of a sort in both Matthew (4:16) and Luke (2:32) where they each refer to an Old Testament passage as explaining the impact of Jesus' coming to earth. As one of my doctoral students has reminded me, you find both the theme of life and light together on the lips of Jesus on more than one occasion

(John 3:14–21; 8:12).[1] But what does it mean to call God or Jesus light? And why is it important?

There are precursors of this in the Old Testament; Psalm 27:1 says, "The LORD is my light and my salvation—whom shall I fear?" This, however, seems to refer to the role God plays in the psalmist's life, rather than a direct comment about God's character.

On first blush, we might assume that "light" in the Johannine vocabulary refers to revelation whereas "life" refers to salvation, and there would be some truth to those assumptions. But both of those assumptions refer to God and Jesus in their *activities*—revelation and salvation are things God *does*. Can "light" be a descriptor of God's very character as well? My answer to this is an emphatic yes, as witnessed in the texts that we quoted at the beginning of this chapter. Let's start with 1 John 1.

LIGHT AS GOD'S CHARACTER

First John 1:5 starts us off with a statement about God's character, namely God is light (cf. Ps 104:2 to Ps 27:1; Ps

---

1. T. Edward Wright, *On the Historical Reliability of Ancient Gospels* (PhD diss., Asbury, 2019, 230).

36:9; Isa 49:6 and Philo *Somn.* 1.75). But a closer look at the texts just cited shows they don't quite say what 1 John 1:5 says. For instance, Psalm 104:2 says God "wraps himself in light," which is not the same thing as being light. Psalm 27:1 says God is the psalmist's light and salvation, and there the term "light" seems to mean revelation or enlightenment. In Isaiah 49:6, it is the servant who is called to be a light to the nations (as was Israel before him). Again, the point of this is that the servant will enlighten the nations—reveal God to the nations. This is not the same thing as saying God is light himself. Notice that in 1 John light is contrasted with darkness in the context of a discussion about human beings walking in light or in darkness where the ethical overtones of those two words are perfectly clear. The Beloved Disciple is not focusing here on God's glory or on God being a truth-teller, but rather on God's pure and reliable character. Not only is God not the source or author of evil or sin, but in God, there is no evil at all.

At this juncture, someone may object and say, "Well, what then does Isaiah 45:7 mean when God says, 'I form the light and create darkness, I bring prosperity and create disaster; I, the LORD, do all these things'?"

The first half of the statement refers to God's work in creation of course (Gen 1). The second half is mistranslated if it says God brings evil. It refers rather to God blessing or God judging human beings—a consistent theme in the Bible. God's judgment is always just and fair, *never evil*.

First John 1:5 is emphatic: In God there is no darkness at all. None! Notice that the term "darkness" (*skotia* in Greek) is characteristic of the Fourth Gospel and 1 John and is hardly found elsewhere in the New Testament (cf. John 1:5; 6:17; 8:12; 12:35, 46; 20:1; 1 John 1:5; 2:8–11 and only in Matt 10:27 and Luke 12:3 elsewhere). In other words, the Beloved Disciple is making a distinct contrast between darkness and light—a dark lord called Satan and a God who is light. Anything that is of the darkness doesn't come from God—be it sin, disease, death. Put another way, anything that is a result of Genesis 3, the fall, is not God's will for human beings either in the order of creation or in the order of redemption.

There is a reason why Paul in 1 Corinthians 15 speaks of death as the last enemy, a reason why so much of Jesus' ministry was dedicated to healing diseases and exorcising the possessed. It is because none of this reflects the character of God—who is nothing but good, nothing but light, nothing but holy in character—nor the will of God for humankind. In other words, we need to stop calling things like cancer "something God gave me." We live in a fallen world, and God, as the Great Physician, is working to overcome sin, death, disease, decay, and, in the end, even suffering and sorrow. This, after all, is the vision of the future presented to us at the end of that last great canonical and Johannine book: Revelation.

This whole line of thinking takes an eschatological and christological turn when we hear in Ephesians 5:14 the exhortation: "Wake up, sleeper, rise from the dead, and Christ will shine on you." This verse comes in the middle of an ethical discussion about avoiding dark deeds, and the sense of this is that Christ illuminates not only one's path but also by being who he is, he enlightens a person about the proper course of action. This would mean that the passage is actually about the spiritual and moral awakening in this life rather than what happens after the future resurrection.

GOD IS IN THE LIGHT

The Beloved Disciple goes on to say that God is in the light (1 John 1:7), and, therefore, we must walk in the light of that light. Even more importantly, in 1 John 2:8–10, we hear: "Yet I am writing you a new command; its truth is seen in him and in you, because the darkness is passing and the true light is already shining. Anyone who claims to be in the light but hates a brother or sister is still in the darkness. Anyone who loves their brother and sister lives in the light." The author goes on to say that such a person has not merely overcome evil; he has overcome the evil one, the dark lord (v. 13).

Notice how light and love go together in this passage. The character traits of God are not only compatible; they are mutually reinforcing. The kind of love our author is referring to is antithetical to sinful behavior, walking in darkness. A person who hates is a person who is not "in the light of God" nor is he or she behaving or walking in the light. The upshot of this passage is to reinforce what we have already noticed: God wants to replicate his own character in us. We are to become like the One we admire, who is love and light.

LIGHT AND LOVE GO TOGETHER— LOVE AND RIGHTEOUSNESS

In fact, it is wise if one considers the character of God by looking at a cluster of related character traits that are mutually reinforcing. For example, since the term "light" has a moral, not just a cognitive, sense when applied to God, we may consider the related idea of God's righteousness.

Despite efforts to make the phrase "the righteousness of God" in Romans 1 about something *other* than God's moral character, that is exactly what "the righteousness of God" refers to in that text. Precisely because God is morally perfect without a blot of darkness in him, he must judge his creatures justly and in righteousness. The positive side of that is God will be fair and will right wrongs and injustices, especially those done to his people. But the other side of God's righteousness, his moral purity, is that he must deal with and must judge sin and evil or else he would not be the God the Bible reveals to us.

Thus, in Romans 1, we see both sides of this coin:

For I am not ashamed of the gospel, because it is the power of God that brings salvation to everyone who believes: first to the Jew, then to the Gentile. For in the gospel the righteousness of God is revealed—a righteousness that is by faith from first to last, just as it is written: "The righteous will live by faith."

The wrath of God is being revealed from heaven against all the godlessness and wickedness of people, who suppress the truth by their wickedness, since what may be known about God is plain to them, because God has made it plain to them. For since the creation of the world God's invisible qualities—his eternal power and divine nature—have been clearly seen, being understood from what has been made, so that people are without excuse.

The wrath of God judging wickedness is but one expression of God's righteousness, and we see this clearly in verses 18–20 above. But that is not the whole story. In light of Christ—the faithful one's salvific work to those who have faith in Christ—God is the vindicator, the one who redeems us or, put another way, who sets us in right relationship with himself.

Scholars have long wondered why Paul would quote Habakkuk 2:4 in this context, "the righteous will live by faith," or perhaps better, "the righteous one will live by his faithfulness," where it seems clear that the word "righteous" has a moral sense in its original context. This raises the question: Who are the righteous in Paul's use of this Old Testament phrase? The answer is those whom God has set right by grace but also through faith. The word "faithfulness" could refer to God's faithfulness in the original text, but in Romans, Paul seems to mean more; those set right by God will live by being faithful to imitate Christ, to live a righteous life, and continue their positive relationship with a righteous God. This makes perfect sense of the contrast with verses 18 and following, which refer to how God judges wicked behavior. This also makes far better sense of Paul's use of Habakkuk 2:4. God doesn't want us to just be in right relationship with him. He also wants us to behave in the right ways—ways that reflect his character as love and light.

JAMES ON GOD AS LIGHT

Let us move on to what Jesus' brother, James, has to contribute to this discussion.

> When tempted, no one should say, "God is tempting me." For God cannot be tempted by evil, nor does he tempt anyone; but each person is tempted when they are dragged away by their own evil desire and enticed. Then, after desire has conceived, it gives birth to sin; and sin, when it is full-grown, gives birth to death.
>
> Don't be deceived, my dear brothers and sisters. Every good and perfect gift is from above, coming down from the Father of the heavenly lights, who does not change like shifting shadows. He chose to give us birth through the word of truth, that we might be a kind of firstfruits of all he created. (Jas 1:13–18)

The unique phrase "the Father of lights" probably alludes to the good gifts God gave us in creation (the sun, the moon, etc.), but the larger context is about godly wisdom for living. James is referring to God giving us wisdom to live an upright and faithful life. In fact, James is talking about how God gives the new birth, new creation to people through his word—the good news of salvation through Christ—which leads to walking in the light (i.e., behaving as God desires). The second paragraph of the quotation reminds us that all good and perfect gifts come from God. This is contrasted with the notion that God tempts us or leads us into temptation or can be tempted, which James vehemently denies. James says no way; God is light, and in him there is no darkness. Furthermore, he is the creator God who, from the beginning of creation, gave his creation light.

Notice the analogy here: Sunlight varies in amount and intensity depending on the time of year, but unlike this, God, who is light and gives light (wisdom/understanding), does not change according to the seasons. Nothing overshadows or changes God who is light; he is constant, and what he wills for a fallen, sinful world most of all is new creation, redemption, and wisdom for living an "enlightened" and light-filled life that mirrors the very character of God.

When sinful desire gives birth to sinful actions, this leads to spiritual death. But when God's desire gives birth to his redemptive action, it leads to new creation. In this passage, James is connecting God's original creation plan, which was entirely good and involved giving good and perfect gifts to his original creation and creatures, with his redemption plan, which again involves giving good and perfect gifts that produce a new creation—new creatures in Christ in an old, fallen world that is passing away. This shows what James means when he says that God who is light never changes. His plan from first to last was to have a world filled with light, filled with goodness, filled with his righteousness and wisdom, filled with new creation and creativity.[2]

THE UNCHANGABLE CHARACTER OF GOD

A few more moments of reflection are in order about the notion that God does not change. What James and other biblical writers mean (e.g., Heb 13—Jesus is the

---

2. For much more on all this see Witherington, *Letters and Homilies for Jewish Christians* (Apollos, 2007; repr., Downers Grove: InterVarsity Press, 2016), 428–36.

same yesterday, today, and forever) is that God's *character* does not change over time. It does not refer to God being "immutable" in the Greek philosophical sense of that term.[3] Obviously, the incarnation, where God's Son takes on a human nature, shows that God can incorporate change into the divine being, but this does not change God's character. On the contrary, the taking on of flesh by God's Son is a manifestation of God's unchanging love and light and his continual desire to redeem his creatures and creation.

Think for a minute about the effects of light, particularly the sun's light, in our world. Without it, human beings could hardly see anything. Without it, there would be no color in the world. Without it, we would never be warm and nothing would grow. Without our sun, soon everything would grow cold and die. Likewise, just as God's love is essential for all of us to live and grow in positive ways in this world, so God's light is essential for our new creation, for our understanding and wisdom, for us to be moral, righteous, faithful followers of God. The character of God, in particular God in Christ, must be replicated

---

3. Which is what the church fathers, deeply steeped in Greek philosophical thought, later debated in the fourth- and fifth-century church councils.

in us as a witness to the world. We are called to be what Jesus is: the light of the world.

It is not for us to hide in the shadows, to withdraw into our holy huddles and hide from our fallen world. We are not called to merely be light-wearers, but light-bearers to a dark world. And like God, we are to be consistent with this godly character. Don't be Mr. Double-Minded, as James puts it, facing one way one day and another way the next, both morally and theologically. We must be consistent in our giving of love and our bearing of light to the world. And this is precisely because God loves the world of fallen humanity, as John 3:16 says, and wants to redeem it. This is expressed both emphatically and eloquently in the Pastoral Epistles in 1 Timothy 2:

> This is good, and pleases God our Savior, who wants all people to be saved and to come to a knowledge of the truth. For there is one God and one mediator between God and mankind, the man Christ Jesus, who gave himself as a ransom for all people. This has now been witnessed to at the proper time. (NIV)

God is love, and God is light; and that love and light is extended to all humankind, though sadly some choose to turn away from the light. Indeed, some love darkness more than light. But what else can be said about God? What other nouns are predicated of him? Next, we must explore the notion that Jesus is the *life*, which interestingly is not said of God in the Old Testament, even though it is implied in calling God the Father "the only living God."

REFLECTIONS

Recently I viewed a partial eclipse in Kentucky. The epicenter for the total eclipse was located three hours from my home, and from our point of view, the eclipse was projected to happen with 95 percent of the moon passing over the sun. However, with 95 percent of the sun covered, only a minor dimming of daylight occurred. Ninety-five percent coverage of the sun did not produce 95 percent darkness as I expected. In fact, if one was unaware of the phenomena, one may not have noticed it. I concluded from this event that even 5 percent of light is still a lot of light! It is true—the light pushes back the darkness and not the reverse. When we consider God as light, we need to truly embrace that there is no darkness in him. His light shines on the life of the believer, and believers are called to reflect his light for the world. And so, as the song says, "This little light of mine, I'm gonna let it shine." Even a little bit of light can push back a lot of darkness.

STUDY QUESTIONS

- What does the noun "light" reveal about God's character?

- What does the phrase "the righteousness of God" reveal about God's moral character?

- What does James mean when he refers to God as the "Father of lights"? What does it reveal about God's character?

- What does it mean to be a "light-wearer" or a "light-bearer" to the world?

This is the message we have heard from him and declare to you: God is light; in him there is no darkness at all. If we claim to have fellowship with him and yet walk in the darkness, we lie and do not live by the truth. But if we walk in the light, as he is in the light, we have fellowship with one another, and the blood of Jesus, his Son, purifies us from all sin.

1 JOHN 1:5–7

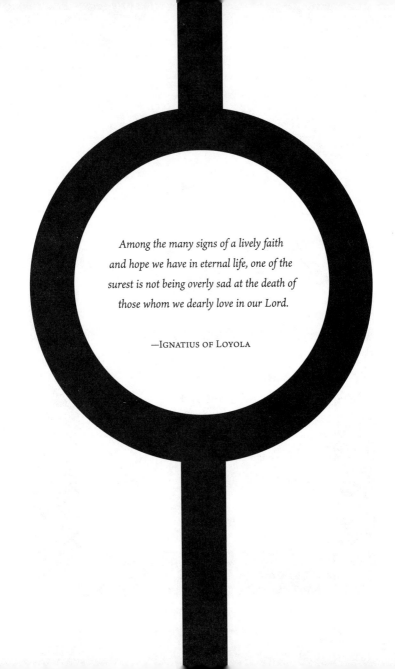

Among the many signs of a lively faith
and hope we have in eternal life, one of the
surest is not being overly sad at the death of
those whom we dearly love in our Lord.

—Ignatius of Loyola

CHAPTER 3
GOD IS LIFE

I was having a conversation with my Old Testament colleague Bill Arnold, and I asked him, "Is God ever called 'life' in the Old Testament?" His answer was telling: "Nothing comes to mind. But that may be because of frequency of usage, since the noun 'life' (*ḥayyâ*) is relatively rare, whereas the adjective 'living' (*ḥay*) is common, with 249 occurrences, as opposed to only 12 for the noun. I'm suggesting they just won't have thought or spoken that way."[1] I agree.

THE LIVING GOD

There is plenty of evidence that God is called "the living God" (for example, Deut 5:26; Josh 3:10; 1 Sam 17:26–36;

---

1. Email conversation on Jan. 21, 2019.

2 Kgs 19:4–16; Ps 84:2; Isa 37:4–17, and I could go on).
Early and late in the Old Testament canon (cf. Dan 6:20–
26) the God of the Bible is called the living God, and the
point is made sometimes over against gods of the nations
who are either said to be real but not gods (i.e., they are
supernatural beings of some sort)[2] or, in some cases, they
are called gods but are nothing more than human-made
idols based on the fanciful ideas of human beings. These
assertions about "the one and only living (or true) God"
comport with the suggestions that this God is eternal—has
always been, exists now, and shall always be.

See, for example, Jeremiah 10:10, where the biblical God
is called both the living God and the eternal or everlasting
King. Daniel 6:26 says the living God is "enduring forever"
(cf. Acts 14:15). It is thus not surprising that in the Gospels
Jesus is called "the Son of the living God" (Matt 16:16; cf.
John 6:69). As we shall see shortly, it is Christ who is said
to be the life, which in this case does not merely mean he is
alive or even just the source of ordinary physical existence
(though John 1, Hebrews 1, and Colossians 1 suggest that
he was involved in creation as well). No, Christ is "the life"

---

2. See M. Heiser, *Angels* (Lexham Press, 2018).

(John 11:25) because he is the one and only source of ever-lasting life for fallen human beings (more on this shortly).

It is profitable to look at other references to God being a living God in the New Testament. For instance, in Romans 9:26, Paul is partially quoting Hosea 1:10, where God's own people are called "sons of the living God"—that is, after they turned back to God and ceased their infidelities. In 2 Corinthians 3:3, Paul speaks of the Spirit of the living God. In 2 Corinthians 6:16, he says we are the temple of the living God—the place where the real God dwells. Similarly, in 1 Timothy 3:15, we hear that the Christian meeting is called the assembly of the living God.

First Timothy 4:10 is worth quoting in full: "That is why we labor and strive, because we have put our hope in the living God, who is the Savior of all people, and especially of those who believe." Here the reference seems to be to God the Father who is called "the Savior of all people," which reflects God's desire that all be saved. However, the writer goes on to say he is especially the savior of those who believe. Initial salvation (sometimes called justification) is by grace and through faith. It's not by predetermination. Hebrews 3:12–13 makes this even more apparent when it warns that believers can be in danger of committing apostasy: "See to it, brothers and sisters, that none of you has a sinful, unbelieving heart that turns away from the living God. But encourage one another daily, as long as it is called 'Today,' so that none of you may be hardened by sin's deceitfulness." Now, there would be no point in warning *all* Christians against apostasy if it was impossible for any of them to commit such an act of turning away from the living God. Furthermore, there is nothing in the text to suggest the warning is just for the nonelect, a warning which would in no way help them if they were predetermined to commit apostasy. No, the warning is for the whole audience. What would be the point of warning the nonelect about apostasy if they had no ability to avoid it? The author clearly believes that the whole of his audience are followers of Christ and they are *all* in peril. They are not eternally secure until they are securely in eternity!

JESUS AS THE LIFE

An important distinction must be made at this point: Only God (Father, Son, and Holy Spirit) is eternal. All other beings have a beginning in time. This being the case, when we are talking about salvation and the life Christ can give us, it is everlasting life we are talking about—a life that begins in this mundane world and continues on into eternity. God in Christ is not giving away what only an eternal being can have: eternal life. Christ is the bearer and giver of everlasting life. Likely this is why we have the phrase in John 11:25—"Jesus said to her, 'I am the resurrection and the life. The one who believes in me will live, even though they die.'" Jesus is speaking to Martha, and he connects the life he is talking about to resurrection—a postmortem experience. His point is that when it comes to salvation or the gift of everlasting life, physical death cannot snuff it out. Indeed, eventually even physical death will be reversed for the believer in the resurrection.

Notice how the various attributes of God's and Christ's character are mutually reinforcing. Jesus doesn't merely give life; he is life. He's the very source of life and, in particular, in this context, everlasting life. The life that he is referring to *must* be received in this lifetime, and it will continue on into and throughout life in heaven and then life in the resurrection when we regain a physical existence. Here, life is connected with salvation, including the final act of salvation when we are conformed to the image of the risen

Lord by means of resurrection. As we saw with Romans 8, God wants to replicate the very character and resurrection existence of the risen Christ in us so that we may be his family—his brothers and sisters.

Another instance of calling Jesus "the life" is the famous "I am" saying in John 14:6—"Jesus answered, 'I am the way and the truth and the life. No one comes to the Father except through me.' " Here Jesus is declared to be *the* way to be reconciled with the Father. The way of salvation equals everlasting life. But he is also called "the truth"—the truth about God, the true revelation of a God who is love and light, indeed, the true manifestation of God in the flesh, such that Jesus can say, "He who has seen me has seen the Father." And yet, he can be distinguished from the Father. The point is he is equally God and perfectly manifests the Father's character and will and love. The clearest revelation of the character of God is seen in his only begotten Son. There is much more we could say about Christ as "the life," which in the Fourth Gospel mainly means he is the source or giver of everlasting life, being God the Son, and so this trait has more to do with his role in redemption than his role in creation, but now we must consider something even more profound and complex: God is spirit.

REFLECTIONS

I've found that the more one becomes familiar with key themes of Christianity, the more faded some of the paradoxes of Christianity may become. For example, consider how paradoxical it is that the death of Jesus is part of bringing forth the way of everlasting life. But as we well know, death did not win. God had a greater plan. Jesus would conquer death once and for all. For this reason, the Christian life is worth living. Paul says, "Where, O death, is your victory? Where, O death, is your sting? … But thanks be to God! He gives us the victory through our Lord Jesus Christ" (1 Cor 15:55–57). For believers, death does not have the final say, as God is both the living God and a God of the living. This explains why we constantly groan for a better life, a different home. We do not live for the destination of a grave on earth, but for resurrection and a new life. As C. S. Lewis writes in *Mere Christianity,* "Aim at Heaven and you will get earth 'thrown in': aim at earth and you will get neither." Or as the songwriter Helen Howarth Lemmel wrote:

> O soul, are you weary and troubled?
> No light in the darkness you see?
> There's light for a look at the Savior

And life more abundant and free!
Turn your eyes upon Jesus,
Look full in His wonderful face,
And the things of earth will grow strangely dim
In the light of His glory and grace.
Through death into life everlasting
He passed, and we follow Him there;
O'er us sin no more hath dominion—
For more than conqu'rors we are!

Christians live with much to hope for in an everlasting life. This is only true because God is love, light, and life.

STUDY QUESTIONS

- How is God described in the Old Testament, and how does this description reveal his character?

- What is the difference between eternal and everlasting life? What does it mean to receive everlasting life?

- What does it mean when Jesus says he is "the way," and how does this relate to the theme of life?

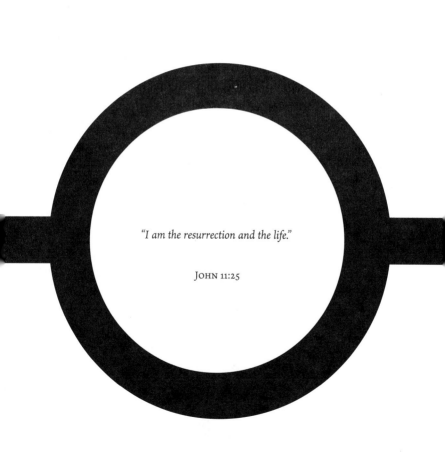

"I am the resurrection and the life."

JOHN 11:25

"Worship changes us into the likeness of the One we worship."

—JACK HAYFORD,
THE HEART OF PRAISE

CHAPTER 4
GOD IS SPIRIT

n John 4, in the context of saying something revolutionary about worship and how it was about to change to comport with "God is spirit," Jesus himself said to the Samaritan woman,

> Jesus declared, "Believe me, woman, a time is coming when you will worship the Father neither on this mountain nor in Jerusalem. You Samaritans worship what you do not know; we worship what we do know, for salvation is from the Jews. Yet a time is coming and has now come when the true worshipers will worship the Father in spirit and in truth, for they are the kind of

worshipers the Father seeks. God is spirit, and
his worshipers must worship in spirit and in truth."
(John 4:21–24)

I take it that when he says God is spirit: (1) Jesus is
talking about the heavenly Father and his very nature,
and (2) he is denying that God's nature involves materi-
ality or flesh. As we saw in our discussion of Hosea 11 in
chapter 1, God's nature does not change in Jesus—God
is not flesh and blood in his very nature. This is what
makes the incarnation of God the Son so astounding.
Why would he take on our very nature? Why would
he allow himself to become mortal, vulnerable, subject
to temptation as a human being? The answer is "for us
and for our salvation."

GOD WITHOUT FLESH ON

The phrase "God is spirit" indicates that God, in his
nature, doesn't have the need of physicality to be who
he is. He does not need a body, physical form, or physical sustenance. Unlike pagan religions, the Bible does
not see sacrifices as providing God with something he

lacks—food, life, breath, etc. He is not missing anything essential by not having a physical form, unlike human beings. He's not like dumb idols made of stone or wood or metal. One of the reasons the New Testament so stresses the resurrection not only of the man Jesus but, in due course, of all mortals is that we *need* a physical form to be all we can be. We have a human spirit, but we are not in essence "spirit" as God is. We are incomplete without bodies, hence the future resurrection.

Bodies are our means not only of self-expression, but also distinction one from another. I have a body different from Sam, who has a body somewhat different from John, who has a body different from Mary, who has a body different from Jane, and so on. With God, it is another story. Mortal bodies change and fail, and creation began that way. God who is spirit does not change in character or nature. God is always the same.

GOD AS SPIRIT AND SPIRITUAL WORSHIP

So why then talk about "God is spirit" in the context of making clear the nature of what Jesus wants to say about worship now that the kingdom is coming? Worship is many things, but one of those things is that worship is the fulfillment of the first and greatest commandment that insists we are to love God with all that we are and all that we have. Worship is the ultimate ethical act. But worship changes when Jesus brings in the kingdom. Kingdom worship does not look like Old Testament worship. It does not involve priests, temples, or sacrifices in the Old Testament sense of those terms. We are the temple in which God dwells. All of us (male and female) are the priesthood of all believers with Christ as our high priest. There is no intermediary priesthood of the few between the worshiper and God in New Testament worship, and the only sacrifices involved are the sacrifice of self, of praise, of service, not a re-sacrifice of Christ. As the book of Hebrews makes abundantly clear, Christ is our one and only heavenly high priest, interceding for us in the heavenly sanctuary after having already become a once-for-all-time, once-for-all-persons sacrifice for sin that puts an end to the entire Levitical system by fulfilling it. Most notably, the sacrifice of Christ even atones for sins not covered under the Mosaic legislation: deliberate sins, premeditated sins, sins with a "high hand" as the older translations put it.

Jesus, in John 4, makes another crucial point; as the kingdom comes, it is not about sacred space (worshiping on Mount Gerizim or on Mount Zion), nor is it about sacred time, a holy hour, *necessarily*. True worshipers will worship God whenever and wherever, for all the earth is the Lord's and any time can be a sacred time and any place can be a sacred space. But the *character* of true worship is to worship "in spirit and in truth."[1]

Notice that it does not say "in the Holy Spirit," though that is true as well. The Holy Spirit indwells all of Jesus' followers and inspires and empowers true worship. Jesus, however, is probably not talking about that in John 4. He is talking about the character of our worship and how it must match the character of our God who is "spirit." So we must worship in spirit *and* in truth, not least because God is both. Jesus himself said he was "the truth."

---

1. The Greek does not say "in the Spirit and in truth." There is one preposition, "in," before the clause covering both spirit and truth. There are no definite articles in the Greek before spirit or truth either. And one must ask, even within the scope of Johannine diction, why Jesus would be talking about the Holy Spirit to a Samaritan woman when he will later say in John 14–17 that the Holy Spirit would not be received by believers until he went away.

I take it that worship "in spirit" refers to genuine, wholehearted giving of oneself to God. Interestingly, this text says God is *seeking* worshipers and, more to the point, this precise sort of worshipers—those who worship God in spirit and in truth. True worship is not merely going through the liturgical motions, though there is absolutely nothing wrong with good liturgy. Good liturgy can facilitate worship in spirit and in truth. Worshiping "in spirit and in truth" is honest, open love of God in an act of corporate adoration. The real emphasis in the Scriptures is on corporate worship; wherever two or more are gathered, Christ is especially present.

But what happens to worship when it varies or strays from the truth? What happens when truth is not proclaimed and not believed, especially the truth about God, Christ, and the Holy Spirit? When that happens, we are in danger of idolatry rather than true worship—something regularly warned against in Scripture. When there is, however, a harmonic convergence of sincere and true worship in worshipers, then God is glorified and the people are edified—caught up in the love and wonder and praise of God.

Worship is the fulfillment of the Great Commandment to love God with all that we are, and it is the avoidance of the fourth commandment prohibiting idolatry. Worship is the ultimate, ethical act of a creature responding positively to the Creator. True worship should lead to morality, just as idolatry leads to immorality (see Rom 1).

Worship in antiquity was messy, involving priests, temples, and sacrifices, and the New Testament is replete with this language as applied to Christ. Probably nowhere is the transformation Christ wrought more evident than in the transference of literal worship language to Christ's literal sacrifice of himself in the flesh. After the death of Jesus, worship had to change as Christ had fulfilled any and all need for such literal sacrifices, and this put priests out of work. But the language of "temple" needed to change as well. The temple is the locus where God dwells. In the New Testament, the temple is, in the first instance, Christ's literal body—he is the embodiment of the living presence of God on earth—and in the second instance, it is the people of God, who become the living embodiment of Christ's presence on earth (cf. 1 Cor 6:19 to 1 Cor 3:16 where Paul affirms both that the individual person is a temple of God's living presence and also that the corporate group of believers together is the temple of God).

The language of offering, *prosphora*, and the language of sacrifice, *thysia* (nonbloody and bloody sacrifices, respectively), are now applied to the crucified Jesus (Eph 5:2). But the Christian life is also depicted as a sacrifice, as presenting oneself to God as a living sacrifice; this is our true worship (Rom 12:1). Failure to do this is a failure to launch, a failure to worship. Have you wholeheartedly given yourself to God? The problem with a living sacrifice is that it could crawl off the altar, which is to say, when we give ourselves wholly to God as a living sacrifice, there is always the danger of desiring to take at least part of ourselves back into our own control.

HEAVENLY WORSHIP BY HUMAN SPIRITS

When we contemplate the worship scenes in the book of Revelation, the saints and angels in heaven are worshiping with reckless abandon. What would earthly worship look like if it was more like heavenly worship? What would it look like if the kingdom had come and we were celebrating that great morning of resurrection right here on earth?

What would happen if we realized that such worship fulfills the intended purpose and life cycle of all creatures great and small? What if Christians should already be celebrating the eschatological victory here and now? It seems to me this is what Jesus is calling for in John 4, however inadequately the Samaritan woman and the disciples understood him. Here are a few other implications that can be inferred from the conversation in John 4: Worship is recognizing who is the Creator and who is not; worship is recognizing who is the Redeemer and who is not; worship is union and communion; worship is not fellowship; worship is a vertical relationship with God, whereas fellowship is a horizontal activity between believers. Worship is theocentric, not anthropocentric—God-focused, not people-focused. Worship is giving glory to God and becoming transfixed and transfigured in the process. Worship changes us, and how we worship (is it "in spirit and in truth"?) affects how much we are changed by it. Worshipers are not an audience, for God is the audience of worship. A consumer approach to worship is not true worship. It's not about giving the people in the pews what they want and crave. It's about giving God what he desires and requires. Worship is about adoration, celebration, jubilation, coronation, and destination all in one. Worship, while it celebrates the past mighty acts of God, should not seek to dwell in the past or make it our main focus. Worship is an act of love, hope, and faith and secondarily an act of remembering. Worship is like a pledge of allegiance; the demand for total allegiance to God takes the form of "you will have no other gods before me" (Exod 20:2–6).[2]

Daniel 7:13–14 indicates that the Son of Man expects to receive everlasting worship and rule. Notice how John 1:51 speaks of angels descending on Jesus and ascending from him. He is not only the Holy One of God; he is the Holy Place, our House of God—Bethel. John 4:23 should be specifically contrasted with Deuteronomy 12:5, where God wants worship to transpire at a specific place of his own choosing. If worship is no longer mainly about atoning for sins (since Jesus completed that task once and for

---

2. For much more about the character of Christian worship see my *We Have Seen His Glory* (Eerdmans, 2010).

all on the cross), then what is New Testament worship about? If it need not involve literal priests or literal sacrifices in literal temples, then what is its purpose?

Worship is a reaffirmation of the intended creation order—not merely the recognition that we are creatures created in God's image (we're *not* God), but perhaps also the sabbatical pattern of one in seven days reflects the restoration of the original creation order (Exod 20:11). But for the Christian, the day of worship is the Lord's Day, the day he rose from the dead—Sunday.

Why is there no Sabbath day in the New Testament? It's not because it's all work and no play now; it's because, in the eschatological situation, it is *all* supposed to be worship, whether involving work or not. It's all supposed to be doxological. All that we do and say should be doxological, an offering up to God.[3] However, "ceasing" from other things is necessary if one is to reflect and engage in adoration, worship. So at times, we need to take a break

---

3. "For the first three centuries the church observed Sunday as the day of worship, but *not* as a day of rest, and the identification of Sabbath and Sunday is relatively late" (C. H. H. Scobie, *The Ways of Our God* [Eerdmans, 2003], 610).

from other forms of ethical acts and rejoice in God and all his mighty works of creation and redemption.

Our worship should be already and not yet, and so eschatological. We celebrate that the kingdom has come in part and it is yet to come in full. Worship now cannot be full eschatological worship. We still have sin and death to contend with. But New Testament worship is a celebration of the eschatological already of Christ's death until he comes again.

REFLECTIONS

Let's return to where we began this discussion. John 4 foreshadows a spiritual form of worship not fixated on this or that location, but rather, focused on the person of God who is spirit, which in turn requires that the character of worship be like the character of God—in spirit and in truth. John 1:14 tells us the Word took on flesh and tabernacled among us.[4] Jesus is the meeting point between God and humankind. He is the source of life and

---

4. The tabernacle was a mobile and ultimately temporary dwelling place for God on the earth in the Pentateuch and early historical books. Here the term is applied to Jesus because he dwelt with us as God the Son for a period of time on the earth.

renewal for the world and the center for the ingathering of the nations.[5] He restores the creation order by redeeming lost humanity and putting it back in right relationship with God. But how is God one if Christian worship has a Trinitarian focus? We must consider that question in our next chapter.

When we consider the nature of God as spirit, the constancy of his character again emerges. He does not change. From an understanding of God as spirit flows the requirement for proper worship—worship in spirit and in truth. So we worship as spiritual beings who are created in the image of God who is spirit. Worship in spirit has one focus alone: a focus on God who is spirit and truth. If this is the case, much reformation is needed in our modern worship services and modern worship songs. The worshipers God is looking for are those who love God wholeheartedly and present themselves fully (body and spirit) as a living sacrifice. This means holding nothing back. This means that worship is daily life; every act of every day is an opportunity to worship. The incarnation inspires worship as we worship the one true

5. Scobie, *The Ways of Our God*, 593.

God who for our sake took on flesh, even though he had
no need of it. This God, worthy of all adoration, is the
one offering living water—water that wells up to everlasting life (John 4:11). All praise and glory are due to
the one who quenches our thirst and conquers death so
that we may live!

STUDY QUESTIONS

- John 4 states God is spirit. How does God the
  Father as spirit differ from humans? What implications can be drawn from this difference?

- What does it mean to worship "in spirit and in truth"
  as stated in John 4? What is the result of worship
  that strays from truth?

- Compare/contrast modern conceptions of worship and worship styles with worship "in spirit
  and in truth." What is done well? What needs to
  be reformed?

- Why does the New Testament lack requirements
  for Sabbath observance? How does this redefine
  the concept of work?

"The Church is the Church in her worship. Worship is not an optional extra, but is of the very life and essence of the Church."

—JAMES B. TORRANCE,
THEOLOGICAL FOUNDATIONS FOR MINISTRY

"Jews focus on the Torah, the embodiment of
God's will; Christians, on an embodied God."

—MEIR SOLOVEICHIK,
"TORAH AND INCARNATION"

CHAPTER 5
GOD IS ONE/UNIQUE

In some ways, we have now circled back to the first chapter of this little study, for the Shema, as it is called (Shema being the Hebrew exhortation to "listen up," which is the first word of our passage in Deut 6) is combined with the commandment to love God.[1]

Deuteronomy 6:4–5 is one of the most familiar passages in the Old Testament and one of the most debated as well. It is the beginning of the direct teaching of God's people by Moses after the revelation of the Ten Commandments. In a sense, this is the bridge between the

---

1. For a much more detailed discussion of this crucial passage, see my *Torah Old and New* (Fortress, 2018). For an excellent discussion of the love command in the New Testament, see V. P. Furnish, *The Love Command in the New Testament* (Nashville: Abingdon, 1972).

Ten Words and the later statutes and ordinances that begin in Deuteronomy 12. As P. Miller notes, the reason Jesus in Matthew 22:40 can say all the commandments hang on the Shema is because, quite literally, the later statutes are the outworking of the love command as given here.[2] In turn, the Shema can be seen as a summary of the Ten Commandments.

Put another way, Deuteronomy 6:4–5 distills the essence of the Ten Commandments and provides the basis for the statutes and ordinances that follow this passage. The Shema begins by dealing with the same issue as the first two of the Ten Commandments and continues by summarizing the rest of them in the command to love one's neighbor. Notice how often we find the language of the Shema juxtaposed with the prologue and first two commandments' language in Deuteronomy (6:12–15; 7:8–10, 16b, 19b; 8:11, 15, 19; 9:1; 10:12–13; 11:1, 13, 16, 18–22, 28b; 13:2–5, 6, 10, 13; 18:9; 26:16–17; 29:26; 30:2b, 6, 8, 10, 16–17).[3] The Shema starts as a confession of who God is to Israel and then leads to a command.

---

2. P. Miller, *Deuteronomy* (Louisville: Westminster John Knox, 1990), 97.

3. Miller, *Deuteronomy*, 98.

Notably, the phrase that introduces this material is the same as the one that introduces the Decalogue, namely "Listen up, Israel." The introduction to the text came to be called the "Shema" because of the initial verb. It is as though the writer wishes to make clear how very important these two pieces of tradition are by tying them together with the same language.

There has been enormous debate about how exactly to translate the Hebrew of the Shema. Let's take a look at the Masoretic Text and then the Septuagint to see two ways these verses have been translated.

> Hear, O Israel: The Lord our God, the Lord is one. Love the Lord your God with all your heart and with all your soul and with all your strength. These commandments that I give you today are to be on your hearts. (Deut 6:4–6 MT)

> Hear, O Israel: The Lord our God is one Lord.
>
>   And you shall love the Lord your God with the whole of your mind and with the whole of your soul and with the whole of your power.

And these words that I command you today
shall be in your heart and in your soul. (Deut
6:4–6 LXX)

Verse 4 is the call to attention and the reminder of the
unique nature of Israel's God. The question is: Do we
translate this "the Lord our God is one Lord" or "the
Lord our God is (the only) Lord" or "the Lord our God
is a unique Lord"? What is the significance of the word
"one"? Does it stress unity or uniqueness or both? And why
would the "unity" of Yahweh even be an issue? Is there
a stress on this God being solitary and numerically one?
The words themselves, *yahweh 'ehad*, as opposed to, say,
yahweh lebad, have led some to suggest since *'ehad* normally has to do with unity while *lebad* has more to do with
uniqueness, it might point the discussion in a particular
semantic direction, but the larger context and historical
situation have to be taken into account as well.[4]

The polytheistic environment in which this pronounce-
ment emerged would favor the conclusion that it was
asserting that Yahweh is the only God, and as such, it

---

4. See Miller, *Deuteronomy*, 99.

would not be a statement about the "unity" or very nature of God per se, but rather a statement that Yahweh is the only living or true God.[5] The older rendering, "Yahweh is our God, Yahweh is One," is on the right track, but it does not settle the issue of what "one" might mean here.[6] D. Christensen, along with others, suggests the rendering of the Hebrew as "Yahweh (is) our God, Yahweh alone."[7] This rendering would not rule out that other peoples might have other deities but indicates that, for Israel, it would be solely Yahweh.[8] Miller suggests: "To confess, therefore, that the Lord is 'one' is to claim that the One who receives ultimate allegiance and is the ground of being and value is faithful, consistent, not divided within mind, heart, or self in any way. The reality of God in one time and place is wholly conformable with all other movements and experiences. … In purpose and in being God is one and the

---

5. See the discussion in R. B. Bauckham, *Jesus and the God of Israel* (Eerdmans, 2008).

6. See P. Craigie, *The Book of Deuteronomy* (Word, 1976), 168, following C. H. Gordon.

7. See also R. D. Nelson, *Deuteronomy* (Louisville: Westminster/J. Knox 2002), 86.

8. D. L. Christensen, *Deuteronomy 1–11* (Word, 1991), 142.

same."[9] In other words, God is unchangeable and consistent in character and actions across all time.

However one renders it, it is clear that this is as close as one gets to fundamental doctrine or dogma for ancient Israel. The relationship between God and his people is exclusive, and Yahweh is a unique deity, who will brook no rivals. When one compares this passage to the Ten Commandments, there is considerable overlap in the exclusivity indicated when it comes to the way God's people are to view, relate to, and worship the one true living God.[10] And so, not surprisingly, when we turn to verse 5, what God requires of his people is exclusive and wholehearted allegiance, love, loyalty, and faithfulness to

---

9. Miller, *Deuteronomy*, 101.

10. Nelson (*Deuteronomy*, 89) is right in saying that there is no general agreement among scholars as to how to translate verse 4 on two grounds: (1) syntax and (2) the meaning of "one." Zechariah 14:9 would support the understanding that "one" means something like "unique"—that is, the only God for God's people. It would not then be a comment at all on God's interior or ontological nature. It is also possible to conclude that 2 Samuel 7:23 provides a clue—the meaning being God is unrivaled and unparalleled: "Yahweh is the one, the only Yahweh" (i.e., the true God). Is this a claim that Yahweh has a unique relationship with his people, or that the other supernatural beings are not truly God, or both? Either way, it would not be a comment on Yahweh's constitutional makeup. The idea, however, entails the notion that the one real God, Yahweh, has given his exclusive allegiance to his people and they should reciprocate.

this unique deity who stands alone in a world thought to be populated by many gods.

The point is not merely that God is the "Most High" or top-dog deity in a pyramid of gods, but rather that Yahweh is the only genuine deity, and there are no other real contenders, only pretenders. This did not prevent either Old Testament or New Testament writers from suggesting that there were other supernatural beings out there (angels and demons, as they came to be called). Indeed, Paul, in 1 Corinthians 10, is quite explicit that monotheism doesn't evacuate the heavens of all other supernatural entities. Paul even calls the pagan deities "demons" (1 Cor 10:21). The point is, they are not nothing; they are spiritually dangerous, and so idolatry must be avoided for very good reason.

The love command in verse 5 is a command to love the true God with one's whole being (cf. Deut 4:9, 29; 10:12). Total commitment is what is implied. This requires not just emotional attachment, but real dedication of the whole person, affecting their thoughts, words, deeds, relationships, work habits, worship, and much else besides. It has been said that the whole of Deuteronomy is, in a sense, a commentary on this verse, showing Israel what shape its love should take, and the shape is law-shaped; it involves keeping the law (cf. Deut 10:12–13; 11:1, 3; 19:9; 30:16, 20, in short, "If you love me, you will keep my commands"). It should be stressed that the language about loving God was not characteristic of ancient Near Eastern treaty documents or covenants.[11]

This is something that is distinct about the nature of the relationship between Yahweh and his people. The injunction to love is based on the prior demonstration of love by God both in creating and in redeeming a people out of bondage. "Heart" here refers to the center of thought and intention, whereas *nephesh* (wrongly translated "soul") refers to the inner self with its emotions and its deepest commitments. The uniqueness of Yahweh as the real God calls for a unique and unconditional commitment by his people, hence all the warnings about idolatry and all the judgments for infidelity.

---

11. W. L. Moran, "The Ancient Near Eastern Background of the Love of God in Deuteronomy," CBQ 25 (1963): 77–87, has shown that the language of love is in some respects reminiscent of treaty language, but when one gets down to specific cases, the language about loving God exclusively is not drawn directly from the treaty terminology. See R. E. Clements, *God's Chosen People: A Theological Interpretation of the Book of Deuteronomy* (Judson Press, 1969), 83.

The love command is treated differently in the Synoptic Gospels. In Matthew 22:24–40 and Mark 12:28–34, the commands to love God and love neighbor are paired by Jesus; in Luke 10:25–28, the lawyer pairs Deuteronomy 6:5 and Leviticus 19:18, which Jesus approves of.[12] Compare other passages—for instance, Mark 12:29–33, where a scribe talking with Jesus reiterates but changes the form: "Beginning with an affirmation ('You are right, Teacher; you have truly said that') and an oddly familiar reference to God ('he is one'), he adds 'and besides him there is no other,' possibly taken from Deuteronomy 4:35. He then abbreviates the four faculties to three by omitting 'soul' and substituting 'understanding' for 'mind,' deducing that this is much more important than all the whole burnt offerings and sacrifices (absent from Matthew and Luke),

---

12. R. B. Hays, *Echoes of Scripture in the Gospels* (Baylor University Press, 2016), 209, suggests that this difference means that Luke is portraying Jesus as bringing no new revelation but simply reinforcing what the teachers of Israel say. Hays's idea has some merit, but isn't quite there. While Luke portrays Jesus as offering an ethic in Luke 6 that does bring new revelation, he also reaffirms some of the standing interpretation of Torah by others. There was partial precedent for combining the love commands (cf. T. Iss. 5.2, "love the Lord and your neighbor," and T. Dan. 5.3, "love the Lord and one another with a true heart"). The form of the double commandment is clearly different in these other sources.

which Mark regards as a wise answer (12:34)."[13] I believe that the scribe here is demonstrating his ability to learn from Jesus yet also to think independently.

What are the implications of this famous passage for our study? Firstly, there is *nothing* in this affirmation that rules out that the one God could not express himself in three personal representations.[14] Although this verse has been taken that way at various points in religious history, as we have seen, the emphasis here is on the biblical God being the true God, the real living one (as opposed to various pagan deities), and his unchangeable or consistent character. Nothing here explains the personal makeup or essence of the one God. Secondly, this is a statement *against* polytheism. God's people are not to worship or serve or obey or love multiple gods. There may also be an implicit message that since the biblical God is the only living god, he is unique.

---

13. S. Moyise, "Deuteronomy in Mark's Gospel," in *Deuteronomy in the New Testament: The New Testament and the Scriptures of Israel* (ed. S. Moyise and Maarten J. J. Menken; London: T&T Clark, 2007), 34–35.

14. In fact, some early Jews understood Daniel 7 to refer to "two powers in heaven," both of which could be seen as divine, as God in some sense. See A. Segal, *Two Powers in Heaven* (Baylor University Press, rpr. 2012), and the discussion in Heiser, *The Unseen Realm.*

By now, the alert reader will have noticed that the nouns we have been talking about (God is love, light, life, spirit, one) "co-inhere," as the scholar would say. We will talk much more about all this in our final chapter, but here is a point worth stressing: Because our God is all these things, he expects us to mirror these qualities in our life and relationship with him. He wants us to have and express love, be the light of the world, be filled with his everlasting life, worship him wholeheartedly in spirit and in truth, and finally, let our loyalty and devotion to him be unwaveringly, singularly focused—in short, "one."

REFLECTIONS

This book has outlined God's character as love, light, life, spirit, and now one. Let's take a few moments to consider what God is not. God is not darkness; in him, there is no darkness. God is not death; he is the one who conquers death once and for all. God is not hate; he is the God who calls us to love all people, even our enemies. God is not flesh; instead, he humbled himself and took on flesh for our redemption. God is not many; he's the one true genuine God. All other gods do not even classify as contenders, just pretenders. A careful reader will have noticed a theme about God's character—namely, it is immutable, unchangeable, constant. This theme inspires trust in God as his character is not a moving target day by day. This theme inspires worship. And so, we have an invitation to worship a trustworthy God. Let us love him with all our heart, with all our soul, and with all our strength.

STUDY QUESTIONS

- What does it mean to claim that the Lord is "one"?

- What are the implications of this claim?

- The theme of God as unchangeable and constant in character is a thread that ties together this study of God. Take a few moments to reflect upon the constancy of God's character as love, light, life, spirit, and one.

- The character of Christians should reflect God's character. Which of these descriptions of God's character is the greatest inspiration to you now?

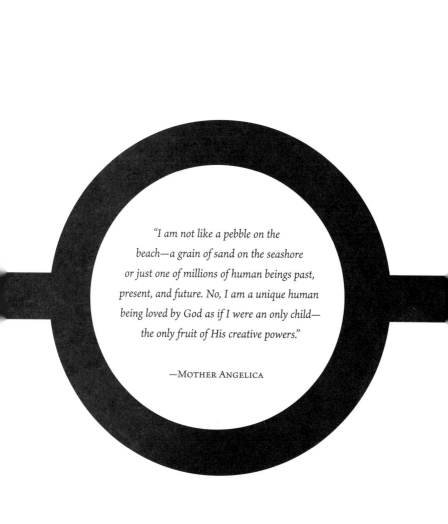

"I am not like a pebble on the
beach—a grain of sand on the seashore
or just one of millions of human beings past,
present, and future. No, I am a unique human
being loved by God as if I were an only child—
the only fruit of His creative powers."

—MOTHER ANGELICA

"Not only do we not know God except through Jesus Christ; we do not even know ourselves except through Jesus Christ."

—BLAISE PASCALE

CHAPTER 6
THE CHARACTER OF OUR GOD

W hen I said that the "nouns" about God's character are interrelated, I meant it. For example, if the God of the Bible was not the only living God (the One), what right would such a god have to demand all worship be directed to him and unswerving loyalty and obedience be given to him? Or consider this: If the God of the Bible was not love—both in character and in action—what sense would it make that he demands we love him with all we are and all we have *and* love all the other beings God also loves?

And if that one and only God has created us in his image, why would we be surprised that love is greater than faith and hope and is the beginning of the fruit of the Spirit? And if indeed it is true this God even expects us to love our enemies, why would it shock us when God has been doing the same thing ever since the fall? Indeed, as John 3:16 stresses, this God loves the whole fallen world and has a plan for its redemption in Christ. And just to make sure we understand that this love is pure grace, Paul punctuates the point in Romans 3–5 by telling us God sent his Son to us and he died for us while we were yet his enemies. Further, when he gets hold of a person, he pours his love right into that person's heart. What kind of love is that, and what kind of God is this? The God of the Bible who is love, light, life, spirit, and one.

Or consider for a minute the connection between that redemptive love and our ability not merely to love God, but to worship him in a new and bolder way. Inspired by God's Spirit, we worship in spirit and truth. Clearly being in God's image has to do with God's character being replicated in us. It doesn't have to do with us becoming gods or us becoming omniscient or all-powerful.[1] Creatures remain creatures, and the Creator stands alone as the only God in the universe. Worship is where we all voluntarily realign

---

1. Here is where the Mormons go wrong: (1) our destiny is not to "become gods" or even "become as gods" (remembering that was the original temptation in Gen 2); (2) God is not lacking anything without a body. He is a self-sufficient being as spirit. The only reason the second person of the Trinity took on flesh was to save us, to be the God-man, a genuine mediator between God and humankind who could represent and relate to both God and human beings.

ourselves under our Sovereign and love and praise him with all we are and all that we have, restoring the creation order and fulfilling the redemption plan to make that happen.

Love requires at least some freedom to respond without coercion or predetermination if that response is to be genuine love. It should also be evident that for the possibility of virtue, of well-chosen good and godly behavior, this requires a modicum of freedom, though it also requires grace, lots of grace. Without grace, no love or virtue is really possible.

While we are at it, how exactly could God be love, be good, if he had predetermined everything that has ever happened in this universe, considering how much evil has happened even in the modern era? Would the God of love and light and life predestine six million of his first chosen people to die in Nazi death camps in World War II? Absolutely and unequivocally not!

The Bible is quite clear in telling us that God is light, and in him is no darkness at all—no shadow of turning. God tempts no one, nor can he be tempted, so unimpeachable is God's character. This being the case, God cannot be the author of evil, even indirectly. That charge must be laid at the door of some other beings in this universe: angels, demons, human beings. God is not the author of disease, decay, and death, sin, or sorrow. Indeed, he is constantly combatting all of that, as is Jesus, the Great Physician and the curer of souls. Think again about the fruit of the Spirit: love, joy, peace, patience, kindness, goodness, faithfulness, gentleness, self-control. These are not only descriptors of the character the Spirit is forming in us; they are descriptors of God's character as well.

God is indeed almighty—almighty to save, to rescue, to help, to heal, to love. But he does not exercise his sovereignty in such a way that other beings in the universe do not have real, viable choices to make in this life. By God's grace, even fallen creatures have some power of contrary choice, though choosing against God is a total misuse of the grace God has given. The very reason God continues to hold his creatures responsible for their behavior is precisely because he has enabled them to make personal choices by drawing on his grace. And this is all the more so for Christians, about whom Paul rightly says no temptation has overcome us from which God cannot provide an adequate means of escape (1 Cor 10). The Christian is supposed to be a person who lives without excuses.

Just as we cannot say of wickedness, "God made me do it," since God rules in our hearts by persuasive love, not by coercion or predetermination, nor can we say, "The devil made me do it," not least because greater is he who is in us, than he who is the so-called ruler of this fallen world. God is not the godfather, making us offers we can't refuse, and the devil is an imposter, a false god, who has no power over the believer unless we give it to him.

What about natural disasters? There is nothing inherently evil about earthquakes, and if, for instance, one happens in Antarctica, we would hardly call it a human tragedy or disaster. It might not even make the news. But sometimes human beings get hurt by natural occurrences. This does not mean that God willed for those people to die.

But there is another side to all this: Human beings have been messing with nature for a long time, and now we are paying for it. Because humans have cut down too much of the rainforest in the Amazon, there are mudslides and other disasters destroying villages and people. Because we spew fossil fuels into our atmosphere, we have been gradually destroying the protective ozone layers, increasing human skin cancer. And that same pollution has led to climate change—extreme swings of weather producing more and more hurricanes, polar vortexes, and melting ice caps. This is not just nature's fury; it is the product of humans destroying the environment. It is caused by human ecological sin. It has been rightly said that humans are the only creatures that foul their own nests, sanctuaries, and homes. Frankly, God will hold us responsible for all our sin, for destroying his beautiful creation, and causing the extinction of so many of his beautiful creatures.

But we are not the only culprits in the perpetration of evil and all things fallen. There are the devil and his minions, and their influence should not be underestimated.[2] It is true that for persons who are "in Christ" and in whom the Holy Spirit dwells there is no possibility of being possessed and so Christians should not make excuses about their own behavior, claiming "the devil made me do it," nor should they blame ordinary problems like a bad cold on demons (for which there is no biblical basis at all). It is, however, true that Satan can oppress, pester, bewitch, bother, and bewilder Christians. He does try to lead

---

2. See Heiser, *Demons* (Bellingham, WA: Lexham Press, forthcoming).

believers astray and to commit apostasy, and the latter is a real possibility. Ever since the garden, he's been trying to lead us down the path to the tree of forbidden fruit. But Satan can only have real influence and power over believers if they allow it. As the New Testament says, "Resist the devil, and he will flee from you" (Jas 4:7). Ephesians 6 reminds us that we are to withstand the onslaught of the devil; we are not called to go on the offensive against him. That's God's work. The good news is that Satan is on the way down. Not only does Jesus say he saw Satan fall like lightning from the heavens, but the book of Revelation speaks of Satan falling from heaven to earth, from earth to the pit (a temporary jail), and from the pit to the lake of fire. Satan knows that he is on borrowed time since the resurrection of Jesus. If even death has been overcome, Satan doesn't have much to threaten us with.

In the beginning, there was only God, and in the end, only God and those who love him will be left standing on the right side of glory. There are everlasting consequences to our beliefs and behaviors in this life, and the sooner we learn that, the sooner we will understand a God who is both just and yet merciful, demanding and yet compassionate, sovereign and yet bestows some freedom on his creatures, loving and yet holds us all accountable in the end for the lives we have lived.

The last sentence lists some of the adjectives that can and should be applied to God, and I have been insisting in this little study that if one wants to understand these traits, one must treat them within the context of the major nouns applied to God in the Bible. This study has not tried to be comprehensive, simply corrective. Obviously, a proper study of what the Bible says about God should include all the verbiage used of God—nouns, adjectives, verbs, adverbs, really everything. What this study is stressing is that the nouns should *norm or guide* the way we look at the rest of the descriptors, particularly the adjectives. Do that, and you will be well on the way to understanding the real character of our one God—Father, Son, and Spirit.

STUDY QUESTION

- Write the nouns of God studied in this book at the top of a sheet of paper. Then write other verbiage used of God in the Bible. How do you see the nouns listed at the top as guiding the other descriptive words used of God's character?

"There is something fundamentally flawed about a purely academic interest in God. God is not an appropriate object for cool, critical, detached, scientific observation and evaluation. No, the true knowledge of God will always lead us to worship. ... Our place is on our faces before him in adoration."

—JOHN STOTT,
ROMANS: GOD'S GREAT NEWS FOR THE WORLD